Bunker Book

by Tristan Trubble

Published in USA by:

Tristan Trubble
P.O BOX #9
Boynton Beach
FL 33425

© Copyright 2017

ISBN-13: 978-1546781493
ISBN-10: 1546781498

Table of Contents

Introduction

Bombs explode overhead, the sound of artillery fire as troops and rebels collide, billowing and suffocating clouds of chemical smoke spreading across a once fertile land laid barren; all while you lie safely below in your underground bunker, waiting for the worst to pass.

Bunkers usually conjure up images of war, but they can be used as a safe dwelling in the event of epic storms, pandemics or even social collapse. Originally, bunkers were created as protective military fortifications to defend people and their valued goods from attack. In WWI, WWII and the Cold War, underground bunkers and above ground blockhouses stored weapons, food and other survival materials and served as command centers for the military. They later became multifunctional, serving as shelters from tornadoes and other storms as well.

Several different types of bunkers exist and their purposes vary. Trench bunkers, for instance, were designed for artillery installations, built out of concrete and dug partially into the ground. Throughout history, bunker systems protected those artilleries ranged around coastal areas. Industrially, their uses have expanded to include housing, material dumps, mining sites, food storage, and even data storage.

Survival from war has often involved underground

protection, from a basic foxhole to an extensive underground system constructed in a mountain, like Norad in Colorado. When Nazi Germany ceaselessly bombed Britain in WWII, the inhabitants regularly sheltered underground or even in subway tunnels. Cellar stairwells, made of stone or brick, were topped with a corrugated metal cover, arched and covered with two feet of dirt. In many cases, bombs landed directly on the house occupied, without affecting those sheltered within the protected stairwell.

When the atom bomb was dropped on Hiroshima toward the end of the war, underground shelters evolved significantly. Not only were air raids a fear, but the catastrophic reality of nuclear war meant that one drop of a bomb could wipe a whole city clear off the map. The US and the USSR stockpiled thousands upon thousands of warheads during the cold war, which propagated so much anxiety that underground shelters became ubiquitous for fear that either country might launch a nuclear attack, forcing the other to reciprocate. This cold war fear lasted between the mid-40s and late 80s.

Cold war bunkers were often buried deep underground, made of corrugated metal and concrete, and were well stocked to supply their occupants for extended lengths of time. The shelters were constructed to protect against nuclear explosions and the resulting radiation. They were also very expensive to install and stock, so only those with deep pockets could finance a personal bunker. However, today the construction, proportions and materials of underground bunkers have changed significantly. Not only that, but modern fears and potentialities have altered as well.

Though nuclear war is still a threat, the potential of such annihilation falls behind those of social or economic collapse, pandemic, terrorism, or natural disasters. Thus, the style of bunker has changed, the proportions have grown smaller, and because nuclear protection isn't the priority, a bunker's construction can be completed relatively inexpensively. That is if you choose to build a bunker in which to survive one of the above-mentioned catastrophes and to store food and weapons rather than a nuclear shelter. The protective properties of nuclear-safe bunkers may jack up the price.

Modern underground bunkers can be located within your home, in many cases below the floor of your garage, which means they can be easily accessed by you and your family and well hidden from view. You may even use your bunker as a safe room in the event of home invasion, or as a storage place for valuables when you're away from your home for extended periods of time. Resistant to flooding and fires, your underground bunker can be the safety net that's there to catch you from a variety of falls.

Whatever your planned uses for your bunker, this book will help guide you in building or improvising your own above or below-ground shelter.

Chapter 1: Why Do You Need a Bunker?

The first thing to ask when planning to construct your own bunker is what catastrophic events are most pertinent to you. If your location is prone to tornadoes, you may need a safe room located underground, primarily for environmental disasters. If you foresee economic or social collapse, then your bunker may be constructed either above or below-ground and will serve you mainly as a protective shelter in which to wait out the instability. A nuclear war shelter will have specific requirements to protect against radiation. You must take these things into account when deciding what type of shelter will best suit your needs.

Environmental Disasters

A bunker will protect against environmental disasters when you need a safe location to wait out the storm. Tornadoes and hurricanes are just two types of environmental disasters for which having access to a well-constructed and well-equipped bunker can potentially save your life.

Tornadoes

Over half of the United States is in a Zone 3 or higher tornado risk zone. Zone 3 includes 200 mph winds and above. "Tornado Alley" not only covers the well-known tornado states Missouri, Kansas and Oklahoma; it stretches all the way from the plains of the Midwest to the east.

Because the potential for this type of environmental disaster impacts so many, installing a bunker for natural catastrophes is one of the primary needs of a bunker. Most know that the lowest interior room of a home is the safest place to be when it comes to tornadoes or other severe weather. Unfortunately, too many homes are built on a slab foundation with no basement. Thus, for most homeowners, an in-ground bunker or storm shelter is the only way to provide the security necessary to keep their families safe.

Bunkers can be built on your own (to be discussed in a later chapter) or can be hired out to companies which specialize in building bunkers. These underground bunkers are constructed with 10-gauge steel, coated with coal tar-epoxy to prevent leaks. They also feature two carpeted benches, and ¼ inch steel ball-bearing sliding doors so that they're more easily accessible when a storm hits unexpectedly. After installation, the bunkers are registered by the company, so that in the event of an emergency, personnel will know where their clients can be tracked and extracted. They will come to your aid if debris has piled atop the bunker's sliding door.

Most bunker models are equipped with battery operated forced-air ventilation, which meets FEMA's ventilation standards ten times over. The installation process usually takes only a day, your home's foundational structure will remain sound, and the dust is minimal, due to the water saw used in the process of cutting the slab. The bunkers are also fitted with a battery-operated weather radio, and an optional battery powered backup solution, which can charge batteries, cell phones, and power laptops for up to 1.5 hours.

Hurricanes

In the event of a hurricane, not only must one prepare their bunker for the natural disaster, but the bunker should be well stocked to face the social chaos that may follow. Looting, fighting, anarchy – many powerful natural disasters lead to varying degrees of social collapse. Medical care and other important services may be inaccessible. Accounting for these possibilities when constructing your hurricane or storm bunker will better prepare you and your family.

The use of hurricane tape in the design of your above or below-ground bunker, as well as in for use in your home, will further protect you and your possessions against the destruction of water damage and damage caused by strong winds. With the record breaking destruction of Hurricane Katrina in 2005, which caused over $100 billion in property and infrastructure damage, as well as resulting in a significant death toll, Hurricane Tape was developed from woven polyethylene plastic. The right-angled pattern of the weave, along with the plastic laminate, makes the tape virtually unbreakable, while the water-based acrylic adhesive, enables the tape to adhere to windows, doors and other gaps into which a storm might find its way. The adhesive is particularly competent at keeping windows from shattering in heavy winds, which minimizes the destruction of your bunker or home and minimizes the risk of injury from shattering glass. Securing your bunker and your home with Hurricane Tape is advisable if you live in areas in high risk of hurricanes.

Manmade Disasters

Social or Economic Collapse

When building a bunker specifically for economic or social collapse, the primary requirements of your bunker would include concealment and secrecy of your bunker's location and existence, and an ample supply of food and water for an unspecified period. The bunker would need to be kept secure from those panicked folks who were ill-prepared for just such an event. Although you could choose an above-ground bunker, the underground bunker consumes no surface area and has the advantage of being kept out of sight.

As with the after-effects of major storms, looting and anarchy would inevitably unfold because of economic or social collapse. While the unfolding events are still somewhat stable, you may enter and leave your home or shelter if it feels somewhat safe to do so. But once law enforcement has been overtaken, and the militia is brought in to reestablish order, instituting a military state in a civilization that is, itself, well-armed, then instability has the potential to escalate to civil war. If you've stocked and secured your bunker adequately, you should be safe from the events unfolding outside your protective barrier, which may devolve even further when public supplies are looted.

Nuclear War

Those who construct bunkers within their home for purposes of protecting against nuclear war, normally build them underground with fiber-reinforced plastic shells to avert above-ground blasts from explosions. Those safe within the bunker should be unaffected by the sounds and physical destruction of the blasts. This means the doors and walls of a bunker must be heavy duty, while still allowing for proper ventilation and airflow, if intended to be inhabited for long periods of time. Additionally, nuclear bunkers must be designed to deflect radiation and withstand the under pressure of shock waves. These protections are easy enough to provide, as the soil and sturdy compact structure of the bunker naturally shields against radiation, while the negative pressure of a blast is often only a third of the overpressure.

These requirements are achieved through superior construction. With a mere 3 psi (0.2 bar) of overpressure, most buildings will cave in; but the frame of a bunker is often built to withstand a few hundred psi (more than 10 bar), which is what makes a bunker bomb- and storm-resistant.

Most bunker plans that are purpose-built involve a powerful structure that withstands physical compression, often made of a concrete arch or vault which is reinforced by steel and fully or partially buried below ground. Those improvised makeshift bunkers may combine previously engineered structures, such as big sewage pipes or transit tunnels. No matter which type of bunker you seek refuge in, the bunker's infrastructure can be shaken by a large ground shock, which has the potential to move your bunker's walls several centimeters in the matter of a few milliseconds.

Most often, purpose-built bunkers are fitted with a trap door, constructed of steel with a steel lintel and frame. In other cases, thick wood can serve well as a heat-resistant door; instead of melting, wood chars. If your bunker is designed with the door on the surface, the door's edges must be counter-sunk in its frame, as, otherwise, a blast wave will lift the door open. A bunker's door shafts can also be used as ventilation shafts. Ventilation and air conditioning are necessary to combat the effects of excessive heat within the bunker. You should fit your bunker with ventilators that are operated manually, as in the event of war, gas and electricity will be in short supply or nonexistent.

The Kearny Air Pump is an effective manually-operated ventilator system. This system protects the vents using blast valves which remain open unless otherwise closed by a shock wave. The treads of a flat rubber tire serve well as blast valves. Secure them to sturdy frames that can withstand the maximum overpressure, and you'll have yourself an effective blast valve for ventilation purposes.

Bunkers may also require weather protection, such as waterproofing from rain. This may simply involve encasing your bunker's structure in a thick 5 mils or .13mm polyethylene plastic film prior to burying it below ground.

The soil will protect the film from disintegrating from sun or wind. You may also need to fit your bunker with breathing tubes and an immersion tub to keep the inhabitants safe from fire storms.

During nuclear attack, the likelihood of death and/or other negative health effects are numerous and the initial effects of a blast are the most fatal. The light, heat, sound, high wind, radiation, tremors, bombs and the fallout of the blast are all intended to obliterate and destroy. A secure, quality bunker should withstand these effects. Let's look at each of these issues in turn.

Light

The first possible effect a nuclear explosion will have is an intense flash of light. This light lasts several seconds and is so powerful that it will instantly blind those exposed to it.

Heat

Intense heat accompanies this light. A wide radius extending from the explosion's center will be aflame. All buildings and all persons exposed to the heat flash will be burned. Those structures made of flammable materials will likely catch fire, but those made to withstand the heat flash will protect all inhabitants sheltered within.

Sound & High Winds

The blast will be so strong that it may deafen those

exposed to it, while a tremendous wave will travel throughout the blast's radius, producing such strong wind and pressure that buildings may collapse.

Radiation

The initial nuclear radiation expands throughout the explosion's radius within one minute.

Tremors

Tremors resultant from the blast are not strong and will affect the structures only a short distance from the center of the blast. Those buildings not destroyed by the initial blast will likely remain unaffected. Those underground shelters must be able to resist ground movement. This would depend on the soil, the bunker's shape and flexibility, and the depth that the bunker has been buried in the ground.

Fallout

The blast will also produce falling debris, as the ground and other structures are sucked up into the air, vaporizing as it rises, and turning into severely radioactive material. This material compresses into tiny particles that scatter with the wind and become imbedded in the ground across wide distances of perhaps hundreds of miles. Though this fallout often cannot be seen with the naked eye, the radiation emitted is like that of an X-ray. The effects cannot be felt, though one may fall sick or die if heavily exposed to the radiation.

Fallout dust continues to be radioactive often for days to weeks following the blast; however, the radioactivity does decrease with time, quickly at first but then more gradually as time passes. In most cases, the radiation's intensity will fall to one tenth of its power seven hours following the blast and to one hundredth of its power after two days. Once this happens, it may be considered safe to exit your bunker for short lengths of time with the right precautions. Though safety gear is not required, you might consider designating some "outdoor gear," like outerwear and Wellington boots, which should only be worn in the radiation-contaminated outdoors and removed before you enter your bunker, so that you do not contaminate the interior of your bunker or your indoor clothing. If you have a radio in your bunker, listen for whether the radiation levels have fallen enough to be deemed safe. In the beginning, you likely will be permitted to stay outside only in one-hour increments. These increments will increase over time, until eventually the radiation levels will be safe enough to remain out of doors. Depending on the strength of the blast, this may take up to two weeks or it may be shorter/longer.

In this book, we will focus on protecting against nuclear war. A bunker that is failsafe against radiation will be well equipped to handle any of the above environmental or manmade disaster scenarios described above. Bunkers provide varying degrees of defense against explosions, heat flash and the resultant fallout. Though the closer you are to a nuclear explosion site, the less likely your bunker will be able to survive the initial effects, a well-constructed bunker will be able to protect those far enough away from the site of origin from the radioactive fallout, which is the primary hazard following a blast.

Chapter 2: Additional Constructional Aspects to Consider

We've already discussed the risk assessment aspect of building a bunker – what are you at greater risk for: natural or manmade disaster? Considering this will help you narrow down the type, size, and construction materials used for your bunker. There are several other aspects to account for, however, when planning for construction: assessing the affordability and geological foundation of your bunker, your survival strategy, the location and entry/exits of your bunker, the bunker's air and ventilation system, and the emergency escape system. You must also know what items you will store in your shelter, and the amount of each required per person. Let's start with assessing the affordability of your bunker.

Assessing Affordability and Geological Foundation

Of course, the investment you make in your bunker will need to fit your budget. Without choosing an affordable option, you will either end up with an incomplete and ineffective bunker or be paying on it for years to come. If money is no object, then a large underground nuclear bunker is your best option, as it will protect against any disaster, manmade or natural. These "stay put" shelters can often involve drastic installation measures, which nosey neighbors will easily spot.

A second, more affordable option is the "urban foxhole" type bunker. Smaller and easily hidden, your neighbors won't even know that it's there, and the option can be installed within a day or two beneath your existing garage.

If you are not financially sound, then creating a simple above ground bunker in an existing room of your home by lining it with plastic and creating a ventilation system, would be your cheapest option. Such a "bunker" or, more accurately, a safe room would serve well in pandemic situations.

You must also consider the geological substructure your bunker will be installed upon. Underground systems may not be waterproof, so building your bunker in porous land near lakes, ponds or rivers may be a difficult – if not impossible – task. In this case, Smart Product Technology's

Security Pod may be the answer, as it's specially designed to be installed in high water tables, is waterproof and rust-proof, and can withstand high pressure. For these bunkers, installation in the floor of your home's garage is the norm.

If your land is made up of hard substrate, like granite or boulders, then you are going to have a tougher time digging out an underground shelter, not to mention higher expense. So, make a geological assessment of your land to estimate construction costs.

Survival Strategy

Another important influence on your bunker's construction is the survival strategy decided upon by you and your fellow inhabitants. If your strategy in the face of catastrophic event is to settle down and stay put for the long-term, then a larger underground bunker for storage and living space may meet your requirements better than a small "wait-out-the-storm" foxhole. One drawback of this strategy and in constructing this style of bunker is that you and your family are basically committed to being static and unmoving. Your reserves and living quarters are quite literally set in stone, even if safe and unaffected life can be found a short distance from your bunker. However, if your survival strategy is to wait out the initial event in a safe place and then be on your way in search of a place with firmer ground, unaffected by the event, then a foxhole type bunker may suit your initial needs – or even your long-term needs – just fine if you don't mind feeling a bit cramped and uncomfortable. But primarily foxholes will allow you to store a small supply of goods and have access to a safe room until you've found yourself an alternative location. In this case, you'll need to have established a safe escape route.

You will also need to identify how many people you will be sheltering, the space required for each, and their everyday dietary needs. Food and water should be well supplied, often with a general minimum requirement of 1200 calories and 10 cups of water per adult daily.

Location & Entry Point of Your Shelter

If you want your bunker to address as many immediate needs as possible, then location is of the utmost importance. All evacuees should be able to reach and secure the bunker within ten minutes.

Underground bunkers have specific location requirements. The best bunkers are located deep in the ground to protect from radiation and debris. Unless your bunker is seriously waterproof, you should locate it outside of areas prone to flood; you don't want to drown in your own bunker. The structure's external walls should be surrounded as much as possible by soil, as the soil provides structural support and protection against heat. You should try to find a location absent from light poles, mounted equipment, storied buildings, and potentially flammable or hazardous materials. And, of equal importance, your bunker should be well concealed.

Secrecy is especially important when it comes to the installation of your bunker. Remember, you've already identified those of whom you'll be sheltering. You've accounted for their supplies and no one else's; so, if any stranger or acquaintance knows of your "secret" bunker then it no longer remains a secret, and the ill prepared will come knocking at your door when the worst hits. Being as much, the location of your bunker is of primary importance, and the installation should be kept under wraps. This will afford you the best security. However, if you choose to install a bunker outside of your property to maintain this secrecy from the prying eyes of neighbors, then you limit your own access to it. In this way, smaller foxhole bunkers installed inside or beneath the home will allow greater access and secrecy. You can enter or exit your shelter as needed, and your bunker can also serve as protection against home invasions. These bunkers can be constructed cheaply, but still offer the lock-system security and ventilation systems required of large bunkers.

The entry system or hatch is one of the most important aspects of your bunker, as it can be built to protect against flood waters, bombings, nuclear blasts, or other intrusions. This may also be one of the costliest aspects of your bunker system. A well-constructed hatch with hydraulic assists can run anywhere from $8,000 to $20,000. Some hatches are built flush with the floor so that they can be better hidden beneath carpet or camouflaged with other flooring. Others are built into gardens or patios and may offer view ports so you can see what's going on above deck. If debris blocks your entryway, some systems, like the Security Pods previously mentioned, even provide a hydraulic lift jacking device which will clear your exit of debris.

Ventilation System

Your bunker is a secure protective shelter, with thick walls and a sturdy hatch. How will you breathe in this containment without some sort of ventilation system or air filter? We've mentioned blast valves before, in relation to bunkers which protect against nuclear radiation. These will prevent pressure waves from affecting your shelter, while snorkel lines should be plumbed with galvanized 40 steel at the very least, to resist blasts and quaking of earth. The snorkel vents should be well-hidden or disguised in a potted plant or otherwise. Store battery and manual backup for your ventilation system, as well as plenty of filters to last however long you anticipate housing in your shelter.

Emergency Escape Route

During WWII, many bunker fatalities were the result of carbon monoxide poisoning after becoming trapped within the shelter. Avoid this hazard by including an emergency escape route, which can either be a second entrance from your primary one (though this can be costly) or a hydraulically lifting hatch, which will remove any debris that's trapped your exit. A secondary emergency exit might be a draining sand hole, which conceals the exit and drains the sand into the bunker when you open it. The downfall of this, however, is that once it's been opened and all the sand drained inside, your bunker will be uninhabitable until you clear the sand out. Emergency exits may also include horizontal escape tunnels, vertical escape shafts, or escape chimneys. The horizontal tunnels usually lead a good distance away from your bunker's main entry to escape any debris. The shafts run through the bunker wall to the outside of the bunker and then vertically up to the surface. And the air- and blast-proof chimneys are built to ¼ of a building's height, at minimum, launching up above the surface through the potential debris. Whichever escape route you choose to install in your bunker, make sure it suits the requirements of your risk assessment.

Chapter 3: How to Build an Improvised Bunker

If you are hit unexpectedly by crisis before you're able to invest in a more permanent and stable bunker, knowing how to build a simple improvised bunker will serve temporary purposes. The design of this shallow-trench structure allows for use of generally accessible materials and can be built within 24 hours. The above-ground part of the structure is sustained by earthen walls, while sheet timber covered with 18 inches or more of dirt serves as a roof. The simple design can protect against fallout radiation and can be further protected with a wall of sandbags or soil is constructed at the same height as the entrance and about two feet in front of it.

Step 1: Choose a location

Your location should be free from water and potential

falling debris and with malleable enough soil to dig your trench.

Step 2: Collect your tools and building materials

You will need several large pieces of sheeting, which could be anything from blankets, sheets, carpets to heavy duty polythene.

You will need a shovel, spade or pick, a wheelbarrow, a screw-driver, a saw, a tape measurer, a knife, 100 2" steel nails and 30 4" steel nails, gloves, and a pen and paper.

You will need timber measuring 2" by 4" by 3'.

You will need entrance and exit doors, as well as a door of about 30" in diameter per person without the handles/knobs. You will also need waterproofing material to encase the doors in, such as shower curtains, polythene sheeting or vinyl floor covering.

You will need pillowcases or bags and pegs and string to create sandbags and mark off the trench dimensions.

Step 3: Mark out your trench

With the pegs and string, mark out your trench's dimensions. On average, your trench should be 36 inches tall, while the width depends on how many people the bunker will occupy (account for 30 inches per person).

Step 4: Dig your trench

The trench should be dug at least 18 inches deep, and the soil should be spread two feet from the trench's longer edges.

Step 5: Construct temporary walls

Allowing 22 inches on one end of the trench for the entrance, construct temporary walls by standing doors lengthwise alongside the trench. Use lengths of timber (40" by 2") to temporarily brace the trench walls.

Step 6: Prepare walls for earth rolls

With the temporary walls in place, use your sheeting material to create a support structure so that you might build the earth rolls against them. The sheeting material should overlap by six or more inches.

Step 7: Construct earth rolls

To form the earth rolls, begin piling your soil on the sheeting material, creating a narrow trench in your soil, as shown. Fold the sheeting material over the earth and tuck it into the narrow trench. Position your next piece of sheeting material and repeat the process twice, so that you've now built up a sturdy protective wall constructed from 8-inch-high earth rolls. This wall should be 24 inches in height. The opposite wall of the trench should only have two earth rolls, 10 inches high, with a total of 20 inches in height, so that the roof will be slanted. You can now remove the temporary structural frame.

Step 8: Form entry and exit frames

Using your 4 inch by 2-inch timber, build one of the frames at 20 inches in height and the other at 24 inches. Both should be 22 inches wide.

Step 9: Place entry and exit

Removing enough earth from your earth rolls to accommodate both entry, exit and sandbags to hold the ends of the earth roll material in place, support the positioning of your entries with temporary earth rolls.

Step 10: Construct roof and waterproof

For the rooftop, place your doors across the earth rolls and cover them with your waterproof materials, tucking the material around the doors. Include an extension in your roof around the entry and exit frames, using 6 inch by 1 inch planks.

Step 11: Cover with earth

Cover the entire structure with at least 18 inches of earth, apart from the entry and exit.

Step 12: Bar the entry and exit with sandbags

Create a barrier of sandbags about 2 feet from each opening, piling the bags to the height of the entry or exit.

Chapter 4: Manufactured Kits & Permanent Bunkers

Manufactured Outdoor Bunker Kit

If the land near your home can accommodate an above-ground bunker, you may purchase a manufactured kit, which will likely contain a structural shell made up of prefabricated steel. A sealed bunker that can often house up to six occupants is constructed by the bolting together of a frame and shell, which is then semi-sunk into the ground and, much like the improvised bunker described in the previous chapter, is then entirely covered by the soil dug to sink it.

Depending upon the manufacturer and the price point of your kit, your materials and construction time may vary. Before you purchase a kit, ensure that the materials are non-corrosive and are virtually indestructible. If you have two-person man power, you may be able to assemble the shell in a day, while digging the trench may take up to a week or even longer.

Manufactured Indoor Bunker Kit

If you have a room within your home that can be converted into a fallout bunker, a manufactured indoor bunker has the capacity to resist the load of a two-story collapse. Often installed in the basement or underground, the bunker protects against fallout with sand, dry-laid bricks, earth bags or other secure materials. Indoor bunkers often allow accommodation for up to four people, while you may be able to combine more than one manufactured indoor bunker kit to boost capacity and add extra storage. With two-person man power, most indoor bunker kits can be assembled in two hours, while the added protection may take 20 or more additional hours to install.

Permanent Bunkers

It is highly recommended to consult or hire a building contractor or civil engineer to construct a permanent purpose-built bunker. Inexperienced builders are not likely to have the knowledge or skills needed to construct a reinforced concrete shelter to protect against explosions and radiation. Permanent bunkers can of course be constructed per your needs and can accommodate any capacity if expense is not an issue. On average, a bunker that is constructed of thick, sturdy materials will offer more effective protection; however, some dense materials are better than others. Below, you'll find a list of materials that are often used in nuclear bunkers. The thickness of the materials is valued to reduce radiation by half. For example, 3.5 inches of slate provides the same level of protection against radiation as does 2 inches of lead. The level of protection can be described in terms of a "protective factor." Your average home, for instance, will have a protective factor of 15, which means that the radiation's strength is one fifteenth less than that of those exposed to the radiation outside. If made of the correct material, your bunker can have a significantly higher protective factor than your home.

For information on the protection value of materials for your permanent shelter and for the differences between each bunker, please see the below tables.

Material Protection Values to Reduce the Intensity of Ionizing Radiation

Increased thicknesses of material reduces the intensity of ionising radiation. For instance, each 0.7 inches of steel halves the radiation intensity, so a thickness of 2.1 inches of steel would reduce the radiation intensity by one eighth.

Material	Inches	Material	Inches
Wood	8.8	Stone	2.2
Slates	3.5	Concrete	2.2
Plaster	3.5	Asphalt	2.2
Earth	3.3	Tile	1.0-1.9
Sand	2.9	Steel	0.7
Brickwork	2.8	Lead	0.5

	Permanent Bunker	Outdoor kit	Indoor kit	Improvised
Approximate Cost	$31,350-$52,250 (more advanced designs will be costlier)	Kit $4,700-$9,400 Not including installation costs	Kit $2,610-$4,175 Not including installation costs	Scaffold frame around $1,300; other materials are scrap
Blast Protection PSI (pounds per square inch)	In excess of 11	Up to 11	Up to 6	Up to 1.5
Ventilation	Forced	Forced	Forced or natural	Natural
Distance for which the bunker will be safe from a one megaton air burst	Closer than 2 miles	2 miles	3 miles	7 miles
Installation	Professional installation required. Takes several weeks to install. Install during peace time.	May install yourself. Takes a week to install. Install during peace time or crisis.	May install yourself. Takes a day to install. Install during crisis.	Install yourself. Takes a day to install. Install during crisis.

Chapter 5: Stock Your Bunker

You must stock your bunker with food, water, medical supplies and protection – both protective wear for radiation or chemical exposure and defensive weaponry.

The following is a list of basic supplies for your underground bunker. The list is not comprehensive but will get you started.

- Radio
- Walkie-talkies
- Flashlights
- Batteries
- Backup manually powered flashlights and radios
- Sleeping bags

- Clothing for the warm and cold
- Candles
- Water-proof matches
- Flares for signaling
- Glow sticks
- Compass
- Halazone tablets for water purification
- Needle and thread
- Skinning knife & combat knife
- Whetstone or file
- Hatchet/axe
- Hand saw
- Shovels
- Fire extinguisher
- Toilet facilities (in a bunker, often a seat set over a deep hole)
- Items of entertainment to pass the time
- 40 gallons of water per person
- Enough food to supply 1200 calories per day per person

These are just a few things to get you started. You will also need to stock up your medical supplies. Below is a basic first-aid kit list recommended by the US Department of Defense.

- ✓ Sterile gauze dressings 10x17 cm (4x7in)

- ✓ Compress and bandage 5x5 cm (2x2in) 4 strips
- ✓ Gauze compress-type bandages 7 cm x6 m (3in x 6yrds)
- ✓ 3 six yard rolls of 2 cm (1in) and 5 cm (2in) gauze bandage
- ✓ Muslin-type compressed bandages 93x93x132 cm (37x37x52in)
- ✓ Gauze, petrolatum 7x66 cm (3x26in) 3 strips
- ✓ Adhesive tape 2 cm x 1 m (1in x 1yd) 100 strips
- ✓ Band-aid 1x7 cm (3/4 x 3in) 100 strips
- ✓ Eye wash
- ✓ Ammonia inhalation solution, aromatic Ampoules (1/3cc,10 units)
- ✓ Povidone-iodine solution, non-ferrous, 10% 1.4cl (1/2 fluid oz.)
- ✓ Sodium chloride (salt)-sodium bicarbonate mixture
- ✓ Surgical razor/scalpel

And, lastly, the following are those medical items not listed in the basic US Department of Defense kit, but which come recommended. Some help treat radiation poisoning.

- ✓ Compazine suppositories (for nausea and vomiting)
- ✓ Antacid tablets (for indigestion)
- ✓ Tincture of opium (for diarrhea)
- ✓ Aspirin (minor pain)

- ✓ Narcotics (major pain)
- ✓ Tweezers

Chapter 6: Alternative Bunkers

Though the bunkers mentioned in this book have been conventional, with a bit of imagination, you can also turn unconventional scraps, shelters or containers into a ready-made bunker. In this chapter, we'll discuss a few folks who have.

Underground School Bus Bunker

[photo credit: wsfa]

For a mere $1,500, James Hunter, a resident of Autauga County in Alabama, created an underground school bus bunker primarily to be used as a haven from tornadoes. After a tornado tore through their trailer park, lifting a trailer from the ground and chucking it across the highway, James and his wife, Claudette, purchased the old disused bus to serve as a refuge for their tenants...and it has served this purpose, several times in fact.

The frugal purchase was manufactured in 1985, and the Hunters found it in a junkyard, buying the old county school bus for $800. They then hired a man for another $700 to excavate the hole. The hole was 27 feet long and 9 feet deep; it just covers the bus, which is fitted with air-vents rising from the ground. The makeshift bunker is a roomy 20-seater, but has a 75-person capacity.

If you're on a budget but have a plot of land, try installing this bunker yourself.

Shipping Containers

[photo credit: martiwf0]

Like the school bus option, a shipping container may also be used as an alternative underground bunker. Wayne Martin constructed his own for as little as $12,500. He first sealed off the freight's double doors and then built a door on one end that opens inward. He then dug a hole that was two feet deeper than the shipping container, and with one foot of space around the back and sides and four feet in front of the door. He leveled six inches of pear gravel at the bottom of the hole and hired a septic tank company to place his container in the hole. He then dug a hole for a 30-gallon perforated plastic barrel to place a sump pump in and built concrete steps from the top of the hillside down towards the foot of the container's doorway. The banks were cut even with the top of the container by a foot inward, and two I-beams were set at the top of the steps level with the top of the container. Other framework was built to support the forms, and heavy corrugated metal was laid across the framework onto the side banks. He then welded re-bar around the opening's rim, equidistant to the holes in the concrete blocks that would be set. He then laid a row of blocks flush with the opening and filled them with concrete. Setting temporary 2x4 bracing under the corrugated metal forms inside the container to support the roof, he installed two 12-inch air vents at the rear and the front end of the container with two inch PVC stubs for utilities. The whole container was then covered with 6 inches of concrete and backfilled with soil. The temporary 2x4 bracing was then removed. The concrete serves as added security; without it, the roof and sides of the container could be pushed in by the weight, or the metal could rust through.

The whole project was done so cheaply, because Martin did most of the labor himself.

In-Ground Pools

Another alternative solution to bunker construction is to take advantage of your already installed in-ground pool. For less than $10,000, you can turn this space into a bunker when you need it most. The requirements necessary to convert your pool into a bunker should be that it meets code, is lighted and has decent drainage, all of which will better serve a bunker's purposes.

The great thing about preparing your in-ground pool to convert into your potential bunker is that most of the structural work is already there. Apart from the partitions and the roof, your walls are structurally sound, and you have built-in drainage. Waterseal the walls and prepare the roof in the same way that the roof of the improvised bunker was prepared in Chapter 4. The rest is done for you. And, even better, the average sized in-ground pool is plenty spacious, which means you'll have higher capacity potential and a good amount of storage space. With the drainage hole at the bottom, you'll also have built-in drainage if there is above-ground flooding, as well as for use as a latrine.

Ensure that your in-ground pool has electricity wired to it, and you will be able to rewire the circuit to a power outlet or rechargeable lighting system. If the power goes out, you'll at least have light enough to find your flashlights if the need calls for them.

This reinforced concrete is already constructed in the ground, so it can certainly do double duty as a tornado or bomb bunker with a little cash and ingenuity.

Conclusion

If some catastrophic event begins to unfurl, you'll need a safety shelter, a bunker, to keep you secure until stability settles once again. When the bombs begin to blast, the artillery sounds as troops and rebels collide, the clouds of radioactive smoke billow and suffocate, spreading across a once fertile land laid barren; you will remain safe from manmade catastrophe or natural catastrophe in your underground bunker.

You know the first step of building your bunker: perform a threat assessment. As yourself for what type of event will you, likely, be using your bunker? Nuclear war, social or economic collapse, pandemic, terrorism, or natural disasters. Next, you'll need to account for other significant aspects when planning your construction: assessing the affordability and geological foundation of your bunker, your survival strategy, the location and entry point of your bunker, the bunker's air and ventilation system, and the emergency escape system. You must also know what items you will store in your shelter, and the amount of food and water required per person.

After these assessments have been made, you'll be able to decide whether you plan to invest in a permanent bunker, an outdoor or indoor kit, an alternative DIY bunker or whether you will simply build an improvised bunker when the time comes. If you choose the last option, you can use Chapter 3 to guide your construction. In any event, you should always have your supplies on-hand and ready to go, including general and first-aid supplies. With a well-constructed and well-stocked bunker, you'll be able to wait out any storm, natural or manmade.